FACING SOUTH

Facing South

Patrick Gallagher

Cló Iar-Chonnachta
Indreabhán, Conamara, Éire

First published 1995 by
Cló Iar-Chonnachta Teo.,
© Cló Iar-Chonnachta Teo 1995

ISBN 1 874700 53 2

All rights reserved. No part of this publication may be reproduced or transmitted in any form or by any means, electronic or mechanical, including photography, recording, or any information storage or retrieval system, without permission in writing from the publisher. The book is sold subject to the condition that it shall not, by way of trade or otherwise, be lent, resold or otherwise circulated without the publisher's prior consent in any form of binding or cover other than that in which it is published and without a similar condition including this condition, being imposed on the subsequent purchaser.

Acknowledgements

Acknowledgements are due to the editors of the following journals, in which a few of these poems were published: *Alpha, Bulletin of Hispanic Studies, The Honest Ulsterman, Manxa, Poetry Ireland Review.*

Published by Cló Iar-Chonnachta, Indreabhán, Conamara, Éire
Tel. 091-593307 Fax. 091-593362
Printing by Clódóirí Lurgan Teo., Indreabhán, Conamara
Tel: 091-593251 / 593157

CONTENTS

I. SUBURBI ET ORBI

1. Just a Moment 9
2. Gaudeamus 11
3. Discreet Charm 12
4. Monochrome 13
5. Dublin Bay 14
6. Chiaroscuro 16
7. August 17
8. Devil Angels 18

II. BEATUS ILLE

9. A.M.D.G. — In Clongowes Wood 19
10. Marine View 21
11. Space 23
12. Drumkeerin 24
13. July Drought 25
14. Corry By Night 27
15. Yuletide Train 28
16. To Medardo Fraile 29
17. Symposium 30

III. TECHNE

18. Cut-Glass Tumbler 32
19. The Latter-Day Rhetor 33
20. Poetic 34
21. Poétique 35
22. Death of a Crab 36
23. Octopus Vulgaris 37
24. Before 1543 38

IV. UT PUPILAM OCULI

25. For Stephen, At Seven Weeks 39
26. For Stephen, On His Second Birthday 40
27. To Catherine Mary, Aged Four 41
28. For Stephen, Aged Three 42
29. Full Fathom Four 43
30. For K.L.G. 44

V. VETULI

31. Closing In 45
32. El eslabón perdido 46
33. Philosopher Vagrant 47
34. Apotheosis Syndrome 48
35. Festive Season, 1976 49
36. Stillorgan 50
37. Public Lectures 51
38. Ruaidhrí de Valera 52
39. Sage Mage 53
40. Lemartinel 54
41. Facing South 55

VI. TERRAE PEREGRINAE

42. Piccadilly Line 58
43. After Wordsworth 59
44. Soho Revisited 60
45. Dog-Day, Argenton-sur-Creuse 61
46. San Bernardo 62
47. A Day in Toledo 63
48. Courtship in Cuenca 64
49. Near the Upper Ebro 65
50. Pastiche Orientale 66
51. Cydonian Alchemy 68

VII. TIMOR MORTIS CONTURBAT ME

52. Timor Mortis (1) 70
53. Timor Mortis (2) 71
54. Apocalypse 72
55. Sic Transit Gloria Mundi 73
56. Summer '73 74
57. Spring 75
58. Curriculum Vitae 76

VIII. IN MEMORIAM

59. In Memory of Philip Larkin 77
60. $\pi\alpha\tau\rho\grave{\iota}\ \alpha\pi o\theta\nu\acute{\eta}\sigma\kappa o\nu\tau\iota$ 78
61. Jesús Ruiz (1935-'88) 79
62. Quondam Fidelis 80

IX. EPILOGUS

63. Cogito 81

I. SUBURBI ET ORBI

JUST A MOMENT

Here, on the first of March,
At Booterstown the breeze is light
And railwaymen in orange jackets
Lark about with ladders.
It's quiet and mid-morningish:
An oystercatcher rising from the reeds
Heads succinctly seawards;
Then nothing, for a moment, stirs.

Under low cloud, soft air
Makes a redbrick house
Across the marsh look near
And newly-built, as though
Now were nineteen-four
And an Anglo-Irish vintner,
Late for work again,
Were in there buttering toast
And ringing horses on the racing-page.

Still no train in sight.
Twin tracks seduce the eye
Downline to Blackrock,
Then up the almost straight half-mile to Merrion
While neat jade water capers
Above the shellbright sand
And new salt fizzes on embankment stone.
This high tide's presence shows
The real absence of
Well-breakfasted Edwardians.
That curious closeness goes.
How many tides? Better not compute.

Raintrailing clouds approach
As drivers, halted a full minute
By the Punchbowl lights, snarl off.
Noise proves we're here,
Keeps the past away
And shuts out thoughts of what we know must come:
Unbreakable silence,
Even less far ahead
Now than just some seconds back
When all the coast-road traffic-lights were red.

GAUDEAMUS

With the climate of Spain here for once,
These old oaks and beeches
Seem to belong to the mountains,
With no suburbs in between.
A sweep of sward to the west
Rises above the ridge-tiles
Of houses skirting the park.
The city down there is a smudge,
Flecked with the sharp light of steeples,
And up in this grass the dew is still young.
The bay relaxes in the sun.
Over the lot the whole sky sings.

DISCREET CHARM

Walking through established suburbs,
Where magpies matrack -ack in garden trees,
And polished parlours, with obscure defiance, meet
The unpractised stupefaction of my gaze,
I think, 'How nice! How in-a-way right they are!'
Till, bemused by the goddess of my mock Arcady,
I feel privileged to amble past sliced hedges,
Like a man who's told he's welcome to meander in a maze.

Yet yonder eastward lies the simple sea,
Accessible in all its amplitude
If apparently horizoned by the sky.
The image brings a foretaste of salinity.
Keeping to declines in the terrain,
I seek issue, as permitted, like a river,
Sensing that a gradual declension,
However indirect, has a purpose in infinity.

MONOCHROME

After a mild winter, at the end of March, it suddenly urned cold,
And on Good Friday morning the snow began to fall.
It seemed another version of the end of the world:
No thunderclaps or cracking firmaments, but the silence of a well.

Darkly from an insignificant sky it fell
And trees assumed the negatives of their prints;
The landscape lost its soundtrack, and the old
Watched young leaves whiten by the hospital wall.

Not that one cannot easily think of worse ways to finish it all
(Or in which it all might finish) than the icing of our sphere,
As those must realise who favour a pretty drift into death, like drowning,
Clean too, slightly dreamy, no fried flesh, no fuss, no smell.

DUBLIN BAY

Cockle shells
That could tell
Architects of Nervi's school
How to build a concert hall
In pre-stressed concrete,
Combining beauty
And acoustics
With engineering skill,
Were much in evidence
On the sand by Cockle Lake.

South a bit,
Towards Blackrock,
The shells were those of razorfish,
The cockles' thinning out.

Farther on,
Near Booterstown,
The razorfish had gone,
And cockles mixed with mussels
In empty unconcern;

Just above high-tide line,
Indecent scraps of wrack
Expired on the buttressed wall
Beside the railway track.

Morning sun
Struck the rim of the bay

As, scanning the strand
From Sandymount to Seapoint,
Alone among the shells,
I heard the daytime drone
Of unwilling Dublin
And, from time to time, bells.

CHIAROSCURO

Observe again the clutter of the mind,
The attic jumble, 'mellow fruitfulness',
Rare-beef sandwiches in speckled shafts
Of lunchtime sunlight;
Elevated fields
Commanding views of cites and of seas;
The ochre earth of Gothic olive-groves;
And real quinces,
Bright and simple as a child's design;
Streams,
The kind that shine when hurdling yellow stones
And gurgle under tranquil humpbacked bridges.

Do we willy-nilly symbolise intent
In typical illuminations
Recurrent as a batch of picture postcards
Held in familiar sequence in a desk
By perishing elastic bands?
Or do signs obscure the dark side of the moon?

AUGUST

Small birds pecking apples as the sun goes down
Rustle me awake.
Looking up, I see among the leaves
The neutral bellydown, the glistened beaks,
And tiepin eyes aglint with dwarfish greed.

The sun is spinning in a hazy sky,
Otherwise immaculate.
Now and then, behind the hospital,
The pitch of lorries changing gear
Disputes the point of writing eclogues here.

Children, too, raucous in their evening play,
Impinge on idylls;
Yet must be recorded as part of a summer's day
In which young sundrunk apples
Are stabbed to death.

DEVIL ANGELS

Jejune perceptions glided through his head
In bright continuality
Telling him nothing they were so discrete.
In the open window of the car they came
At traffic-lights on summer afternoons:
The plated presence of some central river
Slipping under balustraded bridges;
Unseen horses snorting among trees;
A separating cluster of balloons
Released above an ample festive lawn;
And suddenly from nowhere
(Nowhere near a hospital or clinic)
The sweet smell of bandages
And images of wounds
Deep-staunched in a tender bed of gauze.
It was not possible to make a narrative,
Give any shape or sequence to these things
That travelled in a beam of innocent air,
Registered themselves and passed away.

II. BEATUS ILLE

A.M.D.G. - IN CLONGOWES WOOD

I remember as a schoolboy eating daisies
And thinking, 'Well, you could subsist on mush like this
A while at least in April cricket-fields
And avoid the gristle and the soapy spuds
You'd otherwise have for nosh
Each sodding lunchtime.'

It seemed like not a bad alternative
If you chewed them up a dozen at a go:
You could feel the green juice of their stems slip down
Your ready gullet, and the coarser gruel
Of stamen, pistil, petal stick around
On tongue and epiglottis.

It also put you back in touch with things,
Like the farm between the mearing and the river,
Or fording it to unchartable freedoms
Between where you were lodged and tacit hills,
Moon-blue and pap-snug, shutting off the sea
Beyond the capital

Whose sexy neon glow we all adored
At nightfall from our well-appointed cubicles
And thought how soft, how spoilt those people were,
With girls to date and dance with, cinemas,
The pedestrian gloss of lighted pavements,
The warmth of common bustle.

My hunger was as much for that as food
Though it took a lifetime's reading to find out
And I can't even hate the bastards now.
Seems fair to say they simply got it wrong:
Dimness more than malice. Anyhow,
My parents thought my schooldays did me good.

MARINE VIEW

1.
The smell of life and summer at the seaside
Was tides and caves, the mackerel coming in
Like the shadow of a bright Atlantic cloud,
An Indian-ink charge, loud below the waves;
Shale cliffs with spiky grass on top, and girls
You showed off to and got nowhere with
Who laughed when you asked them to the pictures;
The bay all blue and sparkling in the sun
Right out to the horizon where the sky
Rose pale and pearly and indefinite;
Swimming thirty, forty times a day,
Barefoot, free to roam, to probe and sense
Quicksands and dunes, rockpools and surf-sieved shingle;
The evening gust that made your shoulders tingle,
The taut tanned health of smart salt-seasoned skin.

2.
The hills of Donegal seemed far away,
Like the coastline of another continent
Strung out along the north shore of the bay;

Unpeopled, mauve, abrupt and eminent
Above the swell and commerce of the waves,
They noted how the ocean came and went,

Attentive to its rhythms in their caves
Which still fill up with shellfish clicks and clocks
As unchanged tidal bounty scours and laves

The intimate recesses of the rocks,
Smoothing to gems the different-coloured stones
That pit their gloss against continual shocks

And yet remain unfissured, like rubbed bones
Worn rounder by the friction of the breeze
That whittles without edges what it hones:

Thus did large, vigorous, incurrent seas
Pace out the days of dips and ebb-warmed delving
That marked the bounds of our young liberties.

SPACE

For three whole weeks in the Spring
Satellite pictures of Ireland
Were as neat as Egypt
Or the Horn of Africa.

Heading happily westwards,
Hoping the weather would hold,
We swore there'd never been
So much sky above the hedges.

A gulp of that endless air
Was as good as a glass of water;
Midland meadows in the sun
Pleased like simple food.

After a scatter of lakes
Came the black banks of the bog
And, beyond them, small fields full of rushes.
The hills were flat and distant in the heat.

I switched off at the gate
And immediately we heard the cuckoo call
From spruce shot up two metres since last summer.
The air continued, blue and clean and tall.

DRUMKEERIN

Innocence of attitude
Disables the high faces
Of Abyssinian women
In these immediate hills.

No idiom arrests
Young rabbits at play;
Untickled trout
Sleep in slate pools.

Eccentric heifers shelter
In abandoned houses
To escape rain and rushes,
Undrainable fields.

No children now eat
Summer sorrel or berries;
The old people left
Don't even dream,

But mope in grey valleys
That nothing sublimes
Where once a tapped hornpipe
Measured quick limbs.

JULY DROUGHT

Full moon to the south-east,
Over Rossmore.
High cloud: sand banked
On the lake-shore.

In between, thin stars,
A wan blink;
From farm to farm,
Barking bouts; blood-spiders drink

Bramble-blossom dew; Joe Dolan's ass
Brays his plaint:
Unshod, unfed
Celibate saint.

Cattle, parched, pestered
By flies and ticks,
Rub flanks on myrtle,
Fencing stakes, sticks;

Or settle into itchy,
Delirious dreams
Of water over yellow stones
In clegless streams.

In the glum pubs of Dowra,
Meanwhile, men who've mowed
Meadows since dawn
Sink a fierce load

Of Guinness, though some
Sweat and swill shandy,
And all get drunk
As a cure for getting randy,

And brag about hay baled,
Change to whiskey,
Swear red-eyed about trespass
Yet adjudge risky

A decent stand-up fight
With guards about:
Better the nudge or the glare,
Or the single transferable shout,

And the tractors waiting outside
In frog-evicted heat,
And the maledictory ride
Home through ferns and meadowsweet.

CORRY BY NIGHT

In this of course damp place
Where sallies lean towards the racing moon,
The rain gusts sweet and simple from the west.

The nightsunk meadows drink as though
They needed death by drowning; in the flat
Fields by the lake the Shannon brims.

An old man wheezes, spits towards the fire,
Misses, says 'Good God!', feels for his fags
And eyes his sputum sizzling on the flags.

In bright careers among the vacant hills
The rain cascades; the myrtle on The Rock
Scatters mad showers at the wind's behest.

A last light in the sky above the mines
Shows more Atlantic weather on the way:
The low approach, another grand soft day.

YULETIDE TRAIN

Sodden meadows running up to meet my nose,
Red bog, a random splash of pine, then rows
Of sitka spruce behind two curious swans
Herald the raindark pebbledash
Of downtown Mullingar.
In the no-smoking carriage, nuns

Natter a bit in pastoral undertones
And pass each other sainted piggies' bones,
Followed by rustled Mackintosh's sweets.
Rising, I lurch ignobly
Uptrain to the bar,
Swaying by what Spaniards call retreats,

An apple-eating family from Kent,
Smart in winter woollens, men who've spent
So much on booze they can't afford a drink,
Amputated sausages in a
Derelict dining-car,
Menus and trays, an unattended sink,

To halt among heroic alcoholics
(The sort who, urged to stop, just answer 'Bollix!')
With farmers who'd feel nervous sitting down;
And attest the human rites
Of the smoke, the crack and the jar
As sodium lamps glow warm above the town.

TO MEDARDO FRAILE, ON HIS FIRST VISIT TO IRELAND
Glendalough

I know it was a magic place,
The upper and the lower lake,
For you, who drank the whole thing in,
Alert to light and mountain.

But who could suppose that, in the rain,
On a glinting granite trail,
We were to be arrested by
The limpid candour of a lamb?

Straight up to you the creature came
To tell you, with uplifted face,
As you stopped to stroke its fleece,
Something it needed you to know.

You later guessed it sought to show
Us how to find St. Saviour's shell,
Walking along with us until
We strode ahead lest it should stray.

But it was we who lost our way.
The sky grew blacker; we turned back.
St. Saviour's?   Well, another day.
No lamb lit up the track.

SYMPOSIUM
(For Tony Watson)

Somehow staying up till four a.m.
Was normal that one week in the hotel,
As was walking up to Temple Street
Every mild grey morning after breakfast,
On grey pavements, past grey terraced houses,
While the usual grey rain-trailing clouds
Hid all the hills above a thousand feet;

Normal to take a deep draught of that air
And simply feel it good to be alive
In a merry company of friends
Drinking in the gamut of moist greys;
To want to shout or sing and then desist
In deference to those mute blank-windowed dwellings,
Watchful, modest, tranquil, tacit, fair.

Normal enough to slip out to 'The Yacht'
During those morning sessions; normal, too,
To realise that zealous enterprise
Twice at least before the break for lunch
When, back in 'The Yacht' again, the talk would be
Of Sunlight Soap, the charms of County Clare,
Cigarettes, Hispanic prosody.

Normal in the evening to review
The quirks and foibles of each delegate:
The string-puppet stresses of the president;
An oddly-articulated phrase;

The dottier interventions; and the chairman's
Happy gift of shutting people up
With lorry-loads of crude extravagant praise.

Most normal to decide to sing a song,
And do it, among late-night pints and faces,
Splitting the rafters with the lusty sounds
Of the Upper Ebro; inciting dreams
Of bridges, harvests, wine, Iberian pride;
And the unseen, unvisited world so close at hand
All week: woods, valleys, hidden mountain-tops,
Beyond the pubs and theatres, the land.

III. TECHNE

CUT-GLASS TUMBLER

A work of art yourself, you have no need
To be enshrined within a work of art;
Your prismatic clarity decreed
Euclidian effects of part to part.
Such beauty could teach poets how to sing
Of full moons at the bottom of a well,
Or chiselled stars on frosty nights, or Ming
Vessels like a fashioned seabird shell.
Your shivered radiance stings my curious eyes
With fascicles of incandescent spears
That afterglow in inky tracery.
You wound because your rich refraction dies
When all the lights are out, in crystal tears
Of fine-faceted opaque geometry.

THE LATTER-DAY RHETOR

On litotes he was not a little keen;
On anaphora as hooked as any preacher;
Chiastic rigour joy supreme was seen
To give this quaintly dedicated teacher.
About zeugma he would speak a little sadly;
He hated messes like anacoluthon
(Not the sort of stuff to bring up youth on:
You didn't need to train them to write badly).
Dislike of overlap, sense of economy
Overlapped in him and thus he deemed
Polyptoton the most rewarding figure:
More of the same in different forms was bigger
Than mere hyperbole.   Besides, it seemed
Far too many things were called metonymy.

POETIC

Not often in the exercise of style
Is tall polysemy so well achieved
That edifying stories for a mile
Rise skywards, sound in structure, unretrieved.
Nor is it very often that a measure,
Responding to an elevated diction,
Kindles the lanterns of aesthetic pleasure
And shows the truth in artifice and fiction.
The architect of such constructions must
Manipulate an algebra of tensions,
Engineer the medium from the dust
And know the stress and strain of his inventions.
Poets can verify their compositions,
Minding figures, like good mathematicians.

POÉTIQUE

"Je trône dans l'azur comme un sphinx incompris"
(Baudelaire)

Adrift on grey waves, lulled, I sometimes think,
If not of you, of unembarrassed skies,
Blue ever upwards, shrilled by urchins' cries
And plummetting to where five seagulls drink
In candid rockpools darkened by the ink
Of iodine and wounded squid; of flies
Attending marooned seaweed as it dries
Spitting its tantrums at the ebbing brink;
Then see your brightness fill the highest air
With Ptolemaic resonance and space
While freedom takes possession of a mind
Exhilarated by your absent flair
For turning worlds you've never yet defined
Into assumptions of your magic face.

DEATH OF A CRAB

Testing his tentacular tactility
A cephalopod explores the coral reef
Like a cop who hopes to catch a famous thief
And earn a commendation for ability.
Exulting in unrivalled prehensility
He hovers like a breeze-uplifted leaf;
Minor molluscs feel their lives might be less brief
With guarantees of undetectability.
In a plosive submarine turbidity,
Prelude to a serrate radularity,
The crustacean resists its splintered death;
Then stops and dreams with whimsical placidity
Of distant tidal rockpool insularity
As the octopus expresses its last breath.

OCTOPUS VULGARIS

Your complex eyes and saccularity,
Cephalopodal contractility
Define your primitive vulgarity
And self-preserving capability.
When reproductive regularity
Needs equivalents of virility,
Plain tripod hectocotylarity
Proves requisite extendibility.
You are much smaller than you have been painted,
More feared by Man than you deserved to be,
A prey to cod but killer of crustaceans;
Forbears gave up the ink your race is tainted
With by quill-wielders who betrayed the sea
In fabulously idle publications.

BEFORE 1543

Year of publication of Copernicus,
De orbium coelestium revolutionibus,
which demonstrated that the Earth
itself was in motion.

They used to scale sensorial heights
And plunder every planet in its sphere;
They recommended a celestial ear
For imperishable musical delights.
Serenities of Graeco-Latin nights
Sang universal order, while the clear
Magnesium flare of stars made stars seem near
Which, light-years off, were simply burned-out lights.
Plato, Ptolemy, Boethius and the saints
(Superimposition of theology),
Joint authors of this beautiful construction,
Would doubtless have approved of the constraints
Of metre in evoking a cosmology
Doomed by the dawn of limitless deduction.

IV. UT PUPILAM OCULI

FOR STEPHEN, AT SEVEN WEEKS

The happiness of you is knowing wells
And stones which have their places, infant son,
In established quietudes, seclusion
Of mosses, ivy-hung, of ferns and sorrels
Moist-rooted in sprung humus that expels
Tri-atomic ozones, breaths to sweeten
Canopied berries carmined by the moon,
A diligent, sure chemistry.   It travels
Minuscule paths to realise fresh things
With threaded droplets edging to wide days
Of water-linked reflections and dark peace.
We celebrate the oceans of our gaze
Singing each other's pupils; I police
Your lighted depth, meanwhile, to shade its springs.

FOR STEPHEN, ON HIS SECOND BIRTHDAY

My little lexicographer, each hour
Milestones the conquests of your cerebrate day;
At what seems the speed of light you speed away,
Excited by much new-found naming power.
Infans no more, just two, you skirt the moon,
Light up the void, sear clean through astral gases,
Your limpid syntax links galactic masses
By polysyndeton, conjoins a tune
That charms as once the music of the spheres
While deftly, happy dancer, you control
The iridescent craft of human speech.
Those baby joys and terrors, wordless tears
Are already far behind, son, out of reach;
Now the corners of the cosmos are your goal.

TO CATHERINE MARY, AGED FOUR

No image, no, nor figure can express
My joy in you, my flower and my reason
For feeling beauty, zest, a change of season,
Thus apprehending more, instead of less.
Without the candour of your morning kisses
In blossom nudgings of dew-freshened petals
No wasteland of unmarriageable metals
Could match the scrapyard of the life that this is.
Your clear eyes show that gentlest words must be
An insufficient index of affection
Too tender not to be traduced by song;
And yet our love, as simple as the sea,
Abundant, bright, and total in reflection,
Lives here in rhyme, though rhyming it be wrong.

FOR STEPHEN, AGED THREE

What must be kept together by this rhyme
Is you forever and the chestnut tree
You tore across the field to be beneath;
Your chortle as you reached its rounded gloom
And yelled up at its sky-eclipsing green
Wounding its umbrage with your happy teeth
While Catherine, set on staying in the sun,
Loved your whole pleasure and so loved you free
That she recalled for her there was a time
Not long since when she also had some fun
Charging through tepid grasses to unchime
The thousand florets of an elder bloom.

FULL FATHOM FOUR
(To my son)

This afternoon, the shingle at Kilcoole,
Surf-glossed jades and ambers
And ringed obsidian discs
That beach on your unapprenticed insteps
Until the next wave whisks them off again,
Filling all your four years with delight,
At first is just sensational.

Oh, may those brine-neat canted toes
Plunge often into tide-commuted pebbles,
And often those half-anchored heels
Hold hard against the undercurrent's tug!
Testing your strength while having fun's the thing:
The skill you get to add to simple feeling;
And all the waves are different! Looking on,

Until you've fought enough against the keeling
Caused by a bigger roller than the rest,
I pluck you to your mother's chafing towel
And, as you're being warmed and dried and dressed,
Slip wavewards to scoop up for you the best,
The richest pebbles from the foam in crafty hands,
But their shine steams matt in seconds in the sun,
Leaving us a dim psephology:
All greys and buffs and duns, all sea-change gone.

FOR K.L.G.

Our little boy is five. His friend the moon
Is hidden on this February day
By rich north-scudding clouds. I feel the sky

Will gradually clear, and that as soon
As it grows dark our son will see his friend
Laugh through eucalyptus leaves, while I,

Wanting to be with him, hope the fun
Won't quite be over by the time I'm home:
I want to see him eat and drink and play,

Sing solemnly off-key, switch lights off, run
And shout with all his large-eyed jam-faced guests
And nip back to the kitchen to a tray

Of sandwiches and sausages and cake
(For some diminutive voracious pal,
Reluctant to confess he's ever full)

And just before his bedtime, watch him take
The unembarrassed moon from its late height
To set it gently on the garden wall

Behind the eucalyptus tree to light
Packed dreams through a precise dark-scented screen
And beam on his enchanted face all night.

V. VETULI

CLOSING IN

In these warmer nights
That started with the last unclad full moon,
It has felt good
To amble downhill past the Old Men's Home
To the pub
They wish to God they still could have a pint in,
More often, or at all.
The spry ones can, of course,
When they have the price of one,
Like the joker who pretends he's in a flute band
And mince-marches to a twinkling Sailor's Hornpipe
With a wayward jauntiness
In the pale unskimmed iris
That he can just half-see with.
But it's those whose legs can't get them there you miss,
The ones that were always on the road,
Moving that bit slower every time
Till something makes you realise
You haven't seen them since the wet days of last summer;
It's them you miss in case they're not yet dead,
But can't get out to breathe in mountain air
The way they could before;
Enjoy unbounded space beyond the grounds;
Watch buses go by full,
Or win a smile from children;
And are reduced instead,
As the rest of us, should we survive,
Must some day be,
To the best that can be managed
Once decrepitude sets in:
The steps between the TV Room and bed.

EL ESLABÓN PERDIDO
(For Manolo Ferrer)

A simpleton we called The Missing Link
Wore a beret low on his half-inch brow
And was always in the middle of the bar,
Doing..., well, not much:
Sometimes he scratched a dried-apricot ear
With a goose-barnacle thumb
A scholar would at once presume
Was a palaeolithic tool
Or a petrified twig;
Sometimes he squatted on a winecask
And turned his head a little now and then,
As though he had been trained
To supply anthropologists
With a deck of profiles
For illustration in curious monographs,
And had continued out of habit
After they had gone.
Needless to say, he didn't talk or drink,
Nor do we think we ever saw him smoke,
Though once or twice he loped into a group,
Attentive to the boisterous argument,
Shoulders at a stoop,
And knees acutely bent,
As to every point and shouted counterpoint
He nodded mild subrational assent.
But one day, for a minute, Missing Link
Arrested all the banter and the fun,
Seized two wickered demijohns of red
And strode across the square into the sun.

PHILOSOPHER VAGRANT

I walk in suburbs, pondering old dreams,
And hear the world affirmed in children's voices
As points are scored on greens in evening games;
And cadge a pint or two in public houses

And walk again, and crush leaves plucked from hedges
To fibrous pulp whose scent, inspired, springs tears;
Then, frame alight with ale and cosmic bridges,
I fall asleep beyond the punctual stars.

APOTHEOSIS SYNDROME

He practised a precarious bipedalism,
Having reached the conclusion
That the intellectual status
He had accorded himself
Would be confirmed by a shift of his centre of gravity
From the buttocks to the brain.

Rolling on his heels,
He leaned backwards,
A bit more than his embonpoint would suggest was possible
While his head took an even sharper pitch to stern.

And in this commanding posture
He addressed the world,
With everything at a slant,
His apex too distant
To be answerable to mortals.

To be reproved by him
Was like looking up from the base of a pyramid
To a skyful of boulders
Bouncing from the top.

In double-edged complimentary form,
He employed different tactics
Though his anthropometry was the same:
He drained intention from his eyes
And they became as meaningless
As biased slices of gherkin, or
Those holes they put in windowsills to let the rain run out.

FESTIVE SEASON, 1976

Ex-Private Peter Flynn, of Ballinteer's
Old people's flats, at nearly eighty-three,
Shows snaps of his great-grandson's family
And toasts the Royal Dublin Fusiliers
On Christmas Eve in Dundrum House, which smells
Of whiskey and cheroots and steaming tweed,
Then talks of Turks; of capture; being freed;
And stretcher-bearing in the Dardanelles.
"The worst things were the stench in that fierce heat;"
(The rare scratched-bakelite voice and pastel eyes
Are matter-of-fact. He takes a sip of stout.)
"The vultures gorging on the human meat;
Not knowing then or since, with all the lies,
Just what the First World War was all about."

STILLORGAN

Boland's is strictly for the pints and faces,
Old-codger truant crack, nothing hilarious:
The odd half-Wicklow voices of the various
Unhurried crusty topers with wine braces
And navy suits they bought once for the races
At Leopardstown, where bad bets made precarious
What hopes they had of meeting the nefarious
Demands of 'creditors in sundry places.'
Those thin didactic tones and canny grins
In a sweetish warmth of sweat, soiled socks and smoke,
Those unastonishable cockle eyes
Are nudge-and-wink stuff, with a kick on the shins
For fools who fail to crack their kind of joke,
Though a man should laugh, they hold, before he dies.

PUBLIC LECTURES

An old man with a dirty collar
Bent like the north-east corner of a page
Comes to hear new thoughts on learned things.

His two-day bristles glint like quartz
Arranged around an antique grave
While hi-jacked syllables slither on his gums
Like half-slaughtered victims in a sacrificial chamber
Or seaweed slapping in a vacant cave.

And he goes away suffused, convinced
He's been enlightened by a scholar.

RUAIDHRÍ DE VALERA (1916-'78)

He smoked a thousand cigarettes a day
And drank a hundred whiskies every night.
He talked. You played along? He loved to play:
His eyes were grave and brown and Basque and bright
And large and damp and metaphysical,
Roguish, lonely, candid, sly, dismissive;
His attitude to life was gently quizzical;
It was, in fact, except on sex, 'permissive',
If that's the word we're looking for. 'Indulgence',
In the old sense of 'remission', might, however,
Be closer to the world he understood.
It's hard to think of him in full refulgence,
Or even liking it; but he was good,
And knew it wasn't smart to box too clever.

SAGE MAGE

One afternoon, Sakaali came up the hill with apricots,
And made the sun dance on his head above the enamelled sea,
Then slumped into a deck-chair to gaze across the bay
And talk about Damascus, mayonnaise and surgery.

Three donkeys in contiguous fields attended the debate
With tranquil eyes approving both speech and intervention
As when antiphonal cadences assuage a storied hurt
And achieve assembled trust in a provident intention.

The hillside buzzed and crackled its responses to the glare
While Sakaali slowly lit himself a moderate cigar.

LEMARTINEL

You have to be a little lit
To write this kind of stuff
(Difficult to draw the line):-
How, for instance, is my friend Lemartinel?
Does he still, I wonder, live in Jasmine Square?
Polish sentences about archpriests?
Drink a glass of wine?

Or, to be precise,
Does his operative eye
Twinkle over symbols like the sloe
And those emblems of the history of France,
The irreproachably argued
Letters to the press
About the way to say *les haricots?*

Does his venerable head
Attend fatuities with savoured glee
And feed itself another cigarette
In intervals of ancient irony?
Does he, for God's sake, grin these days
When pacing Aquitainian arcades,
Like a polar bear who'd rather not get wet?

I trust my Gallic colleague's still alive,
Observant with that operative eye,
And more amused than bored, as at Bordeaux.
Here's hoping prudent ways
Will guard that shellboned skull,
And hold its seasoned mind,
So that, sagely, it may glow and sagely glow.

FACING SOUTH
Towards the end,

You were happiest in Madrid:
Sun, talk, aubergines,
Cheap scotch and cigarettes

Made it a latter-day Cairo
For you, with Spaniards
As honorary Egyptians.

Even the noise seemed Islamic,
The language you came to too late,
Tongue-clicks, volubility,

Addiction to sweetmeats,
Aniseed, candied fruit:
Just like Zagazig.

Neat labio-lingual
Ejection of salted pip-husks
You observed as a normal skill

In both capitals.
And would muse about this
Between drinks and a dip in the pool.

Out on the balcony
Your wicker chair with the blue cushion
Had to be facing south.

Sitting there last summer,
Nearly blind, you could see
As far as you wanted to.

While we talked, your mind's eye
Crossed all of New Castile
And joined Toledo to Seville

In Hispano-Arab history.
Hearing you, Spanish friends
Felt Morisco blood jump in their veins.

Portugal, to the right,
Was fine, but out past it lay
Greyness, fog. You preferred light.

Heliopolis!
Precise edges at noon!
No shade for the smudging

Revered in the north as subtle
Which you thought obfuscation
(So did Aristotle)

And knew the sun and one river
Made things in Egypt clear.
The Greeks started thinking there.

VI. TERRAE PEREGRINAE

PICCADILLY LINE

Today there was a pretty English girl
Smiling at life, at faces, in the train,
At a picture of bright shoulders in the rain
And gypsy dancers with high heels a-twirl.
Sevillan secrets pleated charms unfurl
Raise ochre incense from the heart of Spain
As jasmine ardours any tart can feign
Make white smoke by the stuck-down raven curl.
She liked the clapped-out world we're living in,
Judging its musty emblems o.k., fine,
Their human victims pets a little bent;
Her candour cleared the air of dusty sin
And we travelled in a fragrance of new wine,
Refreshed, restored, recharged, redeemed, content.

AFTER WORDSWORTH

Boarding a One-Nine-Six in Russell Square
Near the ultimate Victorian hotel
I am transported riverwards with bell-
Signalled pauses by pizza-joint or theatre,
Past the pompous pediments of the Aldwych,
A flash of law-court and St. Clement Dane's,
The swing to King's, then Somerset House's chains
Bracket the dead-straight run-up to the bridge.
There, high above the generous soupy water,
I drink embankment curve, dome, spire (scaled down
By glass emporia where there should be sky)
And, as we hurtle on, stop wondering why
Time should hurtle too, or life seem shorter,
With this lovely sweep of London almost gone.

SOHO REVISITED
(For Geraldo)

In six years
Lisle Street hadn't changed,
Greek Street seemed the same
And Romano Santi's,
Twenty-seven years
Under present management,
Had the same menu, the same north-listing stairs.

Old Compton Street grinned
Like an amiable whore,
A please-yourself-duckie grin
Of polygenous charm;
Or a flaking stage-set
You don't need to repaint
To keep crowds coming in.

Strip-joints come and go
Like hot-dog stands,
And there are perhaps more signs
Of commerce in pornography;
But shabby-genteel Soho
Looks after itself, dear,
And smiles at the resilience of its tawdriest designs.

DOG-DAY, ARGENTON-SUR-CREUSE

One August afternoon
Of meadows, poplars
And a stream,
Near Argenton,

A somnolence
Of insect drone,
Tobacco and warm wine
Languished in the torpor of the sun.

Compliant as hypnotics,
Stunned apples juicened in the dazzled gloom,
And river creatures hung in H2O
Like idle mobiles in an airless room.

The evacuation of colour,
Though swift, was discreet;
A pretty routine
Sort of retreat.

An achromatic stasis
Occurred when this was done:
The world became a picture of itself,
Suspended in the torpor of the sun.

SAN BERNARDO

In the Malasaña district of Madrid
The full moon followed us across a square,
Diagonally, to a restaurant where
The First Secretary had promised us the squid

Was something special. It was. But special too
Was everything that night: food, mood, and wine;
My friends' wives' happiness; and an extra fine
Aniseed haze we ended up talking through,

Till, out in the street again, under mild stars,
Pushing past bands of students whose high chatter
Was proof that where they'd come from there were bars

Still open, we made for one, to be caressed
By lavendered mountain breezes as we climbed
Over sprawled junkies, indifferently dressed.

A DAY IN TOLEDO

I should have taken you to see
Some unlikely synagogue, and had us dream
Away the afternoon;
Or that tall tree
In the cloister of San Juan de los Reyes
Might have done the trick:
You'd have swooned at my exposition
Of Isabelline Gothic; my reasoned
Uuncertainty about the date
Of Santa María la Blanca;
My wit and worldliness; my Arabic etymons!

Why instead did we walk by the river
(You had never heard of
The Prince of Castilian Poets)
Where, with no buildings about, there was nothing to say?
By the time we got back for a drink
To the Calle del Hombre de Palo
The churches were closed and the gold had gone out of the day.

Later, exiled on the other bank, we viewed
The whole thing floodlit on the hill,
Above its honeycombed gorge.
But it was not the same
As stepping through loved wickets
To the cool of blinding gloom,
Or hearing women laugh and chat
While chick-pea stew is stirred for lunch
In sixteenth-century palaces;
Or straying in strong sun
Into cobbled yards where brown girls skip.

COURTSHIP IN CUENCA

That evening we were sickled by a pair
Of streams, and watched, enchanted, hanging houses
Sweep the apricot sky;
A gang of girls across the valley sang
Limpid lovesongs in the murkening air.

Our comportment was objectively correct;
I loved the courtly elegance of your style;
The tender gravity
Of those remarks about my lack of years
Did not show why sound passions should be checked.

Although in their continual percussion
Crickets affirmed some idiom of life
(As did the scent of pine-trees
In the resonant dusk) there seemed
Precious little point in prolonging the discussion.

On the steps of the cathedral, in the sun,
The following day, how bright and cool you looked,
In linen dress and garden-party hat!
Your late eyes said if I'd dismissed the chat
About my age and made a pass at you I would have won.

NEAR THE UPPER EBRO

Starting in discordant elevations,
Tributary streams
Debate among rare haughty accidents
And continual vegetation,
Private in its scents and purity,
Dialect and mere sufficiency,
Its unrepeatable *quidditas*.
Yet somewhere on the way towards the rivers
A brief suspension happens, a hiatus
Between the ruptive uplands
And the fluent intonations of the valley;
A moment, between oppositions,
In which all things are adequately present,
A moment just before *locus amoenus*,
Anticipatory, surrounded by nothing but
The determined declension of all; of all
Mid-foot, mid-metre elements, mid-water,
Preceding resolutions of
Cultivable hinterlands
Tilting to the shade of cities.

PASTICHE ORIENTALE

All day I've feared and welcomed
The closeness of the moon:
Its regular reluctance
To keep its proper distance;
Its grave and awful imminence
Before the sun goes down!

I'll watch it rise above our eastern sea
As night falls on the pomegranate grove.
The idle water-wheels will squeak,
And I'll stop picking jasmine for my love.

Its turn to watch us from the garden wall
Will come later. That is what I fear;
For when my love and I run off to hide,
It will stay near.

Silent, cheeky, with its great dead face
Staring blind,
By saying nothing it will say too much,
None of it kind.

It will mock our joy, our tenderness,
Her roundnesses;
Even if we turn to drink instead.
It is relentless.

And yet its beauty cannot be forsworn.
It must preside.
That is its function and its truth:
Its plenitude.

CYDONIAN ALCHEMY
(For Don Cruickshank)

The honey-apple, quince,
Achieved as marmalade,
Began its sweet career in Greece,
At least as a preserve.

Pouring gold on gold,
They cried "Melimelon!"
And the boiling liquid darkened
And thickened as they stirred.

Latin melimellum
And the metathesis
Of vulgar memirellu
Give Spanish quince: membrillo.

But Portuguese marmelo,
An older form, of course,
When cooked was marmelada
And for that none the worse.

Diffusing the word, the French
Lost its fruit, which is sad,
Though the term is still mellifluous,
Compared with, say, coignade.

The monoglot ambassador
In Lisbon knew he'd got
(When offered marmelada)
Plum, quince or apricot.

"Evidently," he muttered,
"It's a compote of some kind."
If in English it's "of oranges"
Seville doesn't mind.

VII. TIMOR MORTIS CONTURBAT ME

TIMOR MORTIS CONTURBAT ME (1)

Here, in a field, in late October sun,
Four spiders spin to add to what they've spun.

Their filaments, hammocked between blades,
Shine in the sun's grass, shiver in the shade's.

Looking west, immensely late, towards the hills,
I see the sun proclaim the world it fills

With light as one which still requires to live,
Love (and so on) with a bit of give

And take (I turn around) and bla, bla, bla,
Wonder where the hell I've parked the car,

And why I've gazed at spider, grass and thistle
Instead of making for The Pig and Whistle.

My shadow, fully twenty-six yards long,
Describes a man more elegant than strong.

And yet it's not the shadow that is frail
But my substantial self (I start to wail).

We should, but won't, learn (which is why we chatter)
That though material, we do not matter.

TIMOR MORTIS .... (2)

Rarely the world is precious, quite benign,
As on this early mild November afternoon
When a grace above profane, below divine
Shows Spring not far away, though it's too soon
To wish a Winter over which hasn't yet begun:
It must have time to ink its branches on the sky,
But we can't not want to thank the sun, the sun
For lavish light and warmth. That memory
Will dance into flames the hearth's late glow
In flickerings of amber dappled streams
Or stride blazing, uphill, into blackening snow,
With russet, ochre, stubble-gold, fruit-bright dreams.
Odd we should want these props, this rich deceit,
For Winter's truth is spare - and very neat.

APOCALYPSE

To the left of a matt full moon,
In a sky so full of the sun
It was paler than exquisite
Refinements of light blue,
A pictured planet loomed,
Off-white like a well-done meringue,
Its roundness getting bigger
In the simple afternoon.

One wondered how long it would take
This intruder to darken the sky
And show us it really meant business;
As whether the definition
Of its hemisphericity
Would make its plains or craters
Plain or accidental enough
To be plain to the naked eye.

And yet it did seem so benign
In its dogged, objective way!
One couldn't resent it much
For being part of a larger design
Than that which apportioned us
Our moment or two in the void.
Were we really entitled to more?
And, if not, why on earth all the fuss?

SIC TRANSIT GLORIA MUNDI

I eat scotch eggs for sentimental reasons
(Museum Tavern, pickled walnuts, a late date)
And note things like mild days, odd clement seasons
In a half-hearted effort to create
A spot of form and colour in the void
That closes cold around my patterned mind,
Taunting what time has not yet quite destroyed:
In cosmic dust, some day, they'll even find
Crushed temples, bones of antelopes, rare books
Coursing through a wide galactic veil
Towards a farther blackness that will meet
No opposition, stellar particles; and looks
Absently endless. Sable winding-sheet
To which, extinct and scattered, I must sail.

SUMMER '73

The smell of mutton in the hospital
Hung in stairwells on bright afternoons
Where frosted panes
Contained an inauspicious light.

Walking up the steps
One shut out thoughts
Of sub-standard mortuaries
And made an effort to view neutrally
The fact that she would spend her last most gentle days
Ten feet from the air
She loved to respire,
The tall air of Atlantic summer skies.

SPRING

This very heavy April rain
Is sweet - Chaucer was right - yet brings
Back the sour new-life smell
Of all our other springs.

Ever admirable, the burst
Of growth in bud and leaf and shoot
On inky boughs. Until we think
How long ago we saw it first.

The miracle, in middle age,
Can't be enjoyed without unease,
However thrilling it may be
To see it happening to trees.

So when, autumnally, we're spent,
Just frost (and its effect) ahead,
Ruthless, pushy, guzzling spring's
A thing it's hard not to resent

For being so unstoppable:
What's in the way it shoves aside,
And does so every year to show
How time runs out. We'll soon have died.

And now the plants, the little sods,
Burgeon again. But what the hell:
We're only here ourselves because
We made it once against the odds.

CURRICULUM VITAE
Larkinesque

When you're young,
You're really quite a solid little package
Sailing in the universe:
You are, though you don't know it,
Coherent.

Later on,
At thirty-five or so,
Various bits start flaking away,
Drift on their own for a while,
And stick to something in the end
Which isn't you.

Past fifty,
There isn't much of you left,
Other than what you would rather have shed.
So, lumbered with the weight you didn't want,
You shuffle, getting weaker,
Till you're dead.

IN MEMORY OF PHILIP LARKIN
(d. 3rd December, 1985)

Your name, a slightly limp trochaic dimeter,
Well, next to Thomas Hardy's, hardly tumid,
Rings canny-clerkish on the grey perimeter
Of civilised England, where tranquil, humid,
Near-Danish tedium, past toll-bridges and cranes,
Tall between flat wheatfields and the sea,
Shows slums like sepia tints. Elsewhere, the lanes
Are either bulldozed or a JCB
Threatens what's left of all you'd rather save,
Were you not now yourself (alas!) extinct;
But though nobody could 'let you off' the grave,
Neither could anyone link what you have linked
In verse that, from the centre of what's best,
Will smile when Pound and Eliot are undressed.

πατρὶ ἀποθνῄσκοντι

Three sips of brandy and a last cigar
Glow you to language, Egypt, wit; the moon
Is full of Ebury Street, Port Said and Troun
That all the fishes head back to from Ayr,
Absurdly; boyhood summer months in Kerry
Crammed with parched mountains and banana trees
Near Parknasilla; jungle greens; you seize
The images you love; the good are merry.
And all the good, the love you spread about
By loving wife and life so much that others,
Less blessed, the rest of us in fact, increase
(As must this crescent moon you won't shut out)
Shine round you as you make the world your brothers
And, alert to some known sunrise, stare at peace.

JESÚS RUIZ (1935-'88)

Anglófilo, cosmófilo hispanista,
soriano medio abarcelonesado,
discreto ponente de lo ilustrado
dieciochesco español, hasta arabista

en cierne, donamericocastrista,
a lo tonto no, a lo arrebolado,
un arrebol de cielo despejado,
auroral, gongorino, socialista,

en el día de Navidad moriste
entre familia, vinos y manjares,
humano Jesús nuestro: ¡compañero!

Navideñamente a Ágreda volviste,
al calor de tu idioma y de tus lares,
y al pan de un buen mudéjar alfarero.

QUONDAM FIDELIS
In Memory of Pádraic Collins
(d. 26th April, 1995, aged 47)

Holding a glass of red wine up
To catch the sun reflected in it
Shows a ruby glow in a complined nave,
A sign for you once
Of the presence of God
Incarnate there, for a minute

IX. EPILOGUS

COGITO

Out of nothing, nothing.
Out of knowing nothing's there,
Everything.

Feeling emptiness is nothing;
Knowing it is all:
It is the measure of the very void
Which it occupies completely
With perfect knowledge of that absence.
It is pain not sensed but understood,
Clean and individual,
Filling all of nothing with itself,
And every bit as big and blank as God.